EAT LIKE A LOCAL- SINGAPORE

Singapore Food Guide

RIANE FRANCISCO

Eat Like a Local- Singapore Copyright © 2019 by CZYK Publishing LLC. All Rights Reserved.

All rights reserved. No part of this book may be reproduced in any form or by any electronic or mechanical means including information storage and retrieval systems, without permission in writing from the author. The only exception is by a reviewer, who may quote short excerpts in a review.

The statements in this book are of the authors and may not be the views of CZYK Publishing.

Cover designed by: Lisa Rusczyk Ed. D.

CZYK Publishing Since 2011.

Eat Like a Local

Lock Haven, PA
All rights reserved.
ISBN: 9781707867943

Eat Like a Local

BOOK DESCRIPTION

Are you excited about planning your next trip?

Do you want an edible experience? Would you like some culinary guidance from a local? If you answered yes to any of these questions, then this Eat Like a Local book is for you. Eat Like a Local-Singapore by author Riane Franciso gives you the inside scoop on Singapore food. Culinary tourism is an important aspect of any travel experience. Food has the ability to tell you a story of a destination, its landscapes, and culture on a single plate. Most food guides tell you how to eat like a tourist. Although there is nothing wrong with that, as part of the Eat Like a Local series, this book will give you a food guide from someone who has lived at your next culinary destination.

In these pages, you will discover advice on having a unique edible experience. This book will not tell you exact addresses or hours but instead will give you excitement and knowledge of food and drinks from a local that you may not find in other travel food guides.

Eat like a local. Slow down, stay in one place, and get to know the food, people, and culture. By the time you finish this book, you will be eager and prepared to travel to your next culinary destination.

OUR STORY

Traveling has always been a passion of the creator of the Eat Like a Local book series. During Lisa's travels in Malta, instead of tasting what the city offered, she ate at a large fast-food chain. However, she realized that her traveling experience would have been more fulfilling if she had experienced the best of local cuisines. Most would agree that food is one of the most important aspects of a culture. Through her travels, Lisa learned how much locals had to share with tourists, especially about food. Lisa created the Eat Like a Local book series to help connect people with locals which she discovered is a topic that locals are very passionate about sharing. So please join me and: Eat, drink, and explore like a local.

Eat Like a Local

TABLE OF CONTENTS

BOOK DESCRIPTION
OUR STORY
TABLE OF CONTENTS
ABOUT THE AUTHOR
DEDICATION
HOW TO USE THIS BOOK
FROM THE PUBLISHER
1. Street Food Culture
2. Hawker Centres, Coffee Shops & Food Courts
3. Chope!
4. Peddlers
5. Choosing A Seat
6. Choosing A Stall
7. Queuing: A Singaporean Pastime Queuing: A Singaporean Pastime
8. Ordering Food Like A Pro
9. Dietary Restrictions
10. Self-Service
11. Carry Cash In Small Change
12. Do Not Tip
13. Halal Utensils
14. (Don't) Return Your Trays
15. Dabao
16. Open Hours

17. Research, Research, Research
18. One-Michelin Star Street Food
19. A Traditional *Kopitiam* Breakfast
20. Kopi, Teh Or Me?
21. Sweet Drinks Are Made Of These
22. Local Desserts
23. Famous Downtown Hawker Centres
24. Famous Eastern Heartland Hawker Centres
25. Other Famous Heartland Hawker Centres
26. Supper Spots
27. Chinatown
28. Kampung Glam
29. Little India
30. Must-Try Chinese Dish: Chicken Rice
31. Must-Try Malay Dish: Nasi Padang
32. Must-Try Indian Dish: Roti Prata
33. Must-Try Singaporean Dish: Chili Crab
34. Eurasian Food
35. Peranakan Food
36. International Cuisine
37. Local Snacks
38. Fast Food With A Local Twist
39. We Love Our Bubble Tea
40. Haji Lane Hipsters
41. Cafe Hopping Culture
42. Picture-Perfect Spots

43. Beachfront Dining
44. It's Tiger Time
45. Breweries
46. Bottoms Up
47. Rooftop Bars
48. Nightlife
49. Splurging In The Most Expensive City In The World
50. Eat With A Local

READ OTHER BOOKS BY CZYK PUBLISHING

ABOUT THE AUTHOR

Riane Francisco is a Singaporean who spent the first 29 years of her life living on the east coast of Singapore. Like most Singaporeans, growing up in Singapore quickly cemented a life-long obsession with her local favourite food, and the eternal quest to find the best chicken rice.

An Eastie for life, she has recently moved to the East Coast of the United States, where she loves regaling stories of the amazing food she misses from Singapore to anyone who will listen.

DEDICATION

This book is dedicated to everyone who did not want to listen.

HOW TO USE THIS BOOK

The goal of this book is to help culinary travelers either dream or experience different edible experiences by providing opinions from a local. The author has made suggestions based on their own knowledge. Please do your own research before traveling to the area in case the suggested locations are unavailable.

Travel Advisories: As a first step in planning any trip abroad, check the Travel Advisories for your intended destination.
https://travel.state.gov/content/travel/en/traveladvisories/traveladvisories.html

FROM THE PUBLISHER

Traveling can be one of the most important parts of a person's life. The anticipation and memories that you have are some of the best. As a publisher of the *Eat Like a Local*, Greater Than a Tourist, as well as the popular *50 Things to Know* book series, we strive to help you learn about new places, spark your imagination, and inspire you. Wherever you are and whatever you do I wish you safe, fun, and inspiring travel.

Lisa Rusczyk Ed. D.
CZYK Publishing

Eat Like a Local

*"I come here mostly to eat,
because that's what they do here.
And they arguably do it better —
with more diverse, affordable food
options per square foot than just
about anywhere on Earth."*

- Anthony Bourdain (*Parts Unknown: Singapore*)

Singapore is a tiny island-nation nestled in the southern tip of the Malay Peninsula in Southeast Asia that enjoys (or suffers from, depending on who you ask) hot, humid tropical weather all year around.

First established as a trading port in 1819, it was once a British colony before merging with Malaya in 1963 after the Japanese occupation. After becoming an independent country in 1965, the tiny city-state of Singapore has since grown from a third-world nation to first-world.

While portrayed as a glitzy luxurious homeland of spoilt rich billionaires in the recent Hollywood hit Crazy Rich Asians, a majority of Singaporeans are actually of the middle-income class and live in public housing, otherwise known as the Housing Development Board (HDB) flats. A multi-cultural nation made from immigrants from around the region, the population is predominantly Chinese, followed by

Malay, Indian and other races. While Malay is the national language of Singapore, English is the official language used nation-wide, although Mandarin and Chinese dialects are widely spoken due to the Chinese majority.

A booming financial and job market have also seen a recent influx of immigrants from around the world, turning Singapore into an increasingly cosmopolitan and globalised society. Renowned for its safety, efficiency, and cleanliness but infamous for its strict laws and fines, it represents a prosperous haven of opportunity for some and a repressive, sterile utopia for others. But despite our nation's quirks and flaws, the one thing that unites us all Singaporeans is our undeniable love for local food.

For Singaporeans, food is often more than just a meal. Often used as social glue, many important occasions are often celebrated through food, a constant across all the different ethnicities in Singapore. A mix of high-end and cheap establishments are also found throughout the island, ensuring a good meal to be found for everyone, no matter the size of the wallet. Singapore's local cuisine is one of our major attractions, heavily exalted by both the local tourism board as well as Singaporeans, with hawker centres arguably the most prominent of the thriving food scene.

The tips in this book are not an exhaustive list, and definitely not **the** definitive list, especially when describing a local food heritage as multifaceted and complex as Singapore's. Instead, take these tips as a fun introduction to the eclectic and vibrant food scene in Singapore. Food is something held close to every Singaporean's heart, and fierce debates have been held over the years over where best dishes can be found.

So by all means, use the stalls, restaurants, and bars in this book as a personal recommendation from me to you, but be sure to ask other locals when you can too. And most of all, keep an open mind as you eat your way around Singapore and hope you have as much fun as I do exploring this tiny sunny island I still call home.

Singapore

Singapore Climate

	High	Low
January	87	76
February	88	76
March	90	77
April	90	78
May	90	79
June	89	78
July	88	78
August	88	78
September	88	78
October	89	78
November	88	77
December	87	76

GreaterThanaTourist.com

Temperatures are in Fahrenheit degrees.
Source: NOAA

Eat Like a Local

1. STREET FOOD CULTURE

The backbone of Singapore's food culture is undisputedly its street food. But in a country that prides itself on cleanliness and strict urban planning, a huge overhaul to the street food scene was done in the 1960s. Since then stalls have been licensed and neatly contained in hawker centres, shops or food courts, resulting in more than a hundred hawker centres across the tiny island today!

The food served from stall to stall vary greatly, each one specialising in just a few dishes. Many of these dishes evolved from original cuisines brought over by early immigrants such as the Chinese, Malay and Indians, and have become beloved staples of Singaporeans across all races.

Many popular stalls have been around for years, passed through generations by the stall's cooks, also known as hawkers. Unfortunately, hawkers are an ageing breed, and with younger generations shying away from blue-collar jobs due to Singapore's growing affluence, the local government has poured millions of dollars into promoting and continuing the hawker culture, hopefully for many years to come.

2. HAWKER CENTRES, COFFEE SHOPS & FOOD COURTS

Hawker centres are larger open-air stand-alone establishments found throughout the island, housing multiple rows of stalls with tables and chairs arranged in between them for patrons.

Coffee shops (not to be confused with cafes), are best described as eating houses and are smaller versions of hawker centres with typically just one row of several food stalls and a drink stall. Also colloquially called *kopitiams,* they're often situated at the void decks of HDB flats.

Food courts tend to be smaller than hawker centres, are air-conditioned and often found in almost every shopping mall in Singapore. Food prices in food courts also tend to be higher, especially in malls downtown.

Eat Like a Local

While all of them are heavily patronised by locals throughout the day, the next few tips focus on hawker centres as that is where most of the renowned stalls can be found.

3. CHOPE!

The first time at a hawker centre can be an overwhelming experience. It's hot, loud, and crowded. You're about to sit down with a plate of food you just bought when you realise that every seat is occupied by either a person or.. a packet of tissue paper??

To *chope* (Singlish for reserve) a table or seat before buying your meal is an unspoken rule at hawker centres. During peak hours, securing a seat is a priority unless one wants to risk getting their food cold or wasting their precious lunch hour in search of a seat. As such, it has become common local knowledge that announcing a seat as *choped* is done best with an inexpensive packet of tissue paper, although name cards, staff passes, umbrellas and plastic bags are also used.

This *chope* culture has both its share of supporters, who admire Singaporeans for their ingenuity and unapologetic practicality and its detractors, who dismiss it as selfish inconsideration.

Whatever either may say, *chope*-ing continues to work. So next time you're at a hawker centre, try to *chope* a seat first, and remember to take note of your table number (see Tip 10. Self Service)

4. PEDDLERS

Ready to chope a table, but need a tissue packet? Tissue paper sellers (also known as tissue aunties or uncles as they tend to be elderly, needy folk) are a common sight in hawker centres, as they try to sell their packets from table to table. Although it is technically illegal to peddle in hawker centres, these sellers still do so as locals do buy their tissue packets, sometimes out of sympathy, often out of convenience.

Although far less common, you may come across other peddlers who sell trinkets, often accompanied by a document of some sort citing disability or financial difficulties. While it is really up to you to decide to buy from any peddler, do remember you're not obliged to do so. Like many locals do, a simple wave and a 'no thank you' will suffice, but if a peddler is particularly insistent, ignoring them tends to work.

5. CHOOSING A SEAT

Most hawker centres practise free seating, leaving you free to sit wherever you find space, regardless of whichever stall you eat from. Sharing a table with strangers is common practice, so feel free to ask people if a seat is taken before you *chope* a seat.

Tables are also numbered, as some stalls delivering the food to your table, so do take note of your table number after you *chope* your seat. However, in more touristy hawker centres, some stalls do designate several tables in front of their stall just for their customers, *chope*-ing these tables with a table cloth or menus.

Do also look out for touts. While illegal, relentless pushy stall owners may sometimes harass you to order from their stalls, or try to bring you to their designated seating and often overcharge for their food. Locals tend to steer clear of these stalls; the best stalls are often too busy to have time to tout. A simple no thank you while walking away should do the trick if you encounter one.

6. CHOOSING A STALL

Unless you already have a recommended stall you intend to try, it's best to take a lap around the hawker centre to look at your different options. And if you can't decide on just one, feel free to order food from more than one stall! It's easy to have a feast for cheap in hawker centres as most typical basic meals are priced around $3-$7.

Hygiene checks are routinely carried out in each stall, and the rating A, B, C or D displayed prominently on stall fronts. Locals do not pay too much attention to these ratings as some of the best food can be found in C-rated stalls, and many locals

Eat Like a Local

are more than happy to sacrifice a little hygiene in the pursuit of a delicious bowl of noodles.

Halal food for Muslims can also readily be found in hawker centres, and halal stalls are indicated by a halal-certified sticker on their signboard. Typically, these stalls are owned by Muslim hawkers and typically serve Malay and Southern Indian cuisine. (See Tip 13. Halal Utensils)

And if you're looking for the best food in the centre, be sure to read the next tip.

7. QUEUING: A SINGAPOREAN PASTIME QUEUING: A SINGAPOREAN PASTIME

Cram almost six million people in a tiny island of about 720km^2, and it's easy to understand why queuing is common here, especially for sales, transport or food.

And while we Singaporeans are generally an impatient bunch (social media explodes with complaints whenever there are MRT delays or breakdowns), we make an exception for good food. So when choosing a stall, try to pick one with a queue, or better yet a snaking queue because chances are it serves great food that is popular with locals.

Hate queues? Avoid the lunch rush from 12-1.30pm when hordes of office workers descend upon nearby hawker centres for a quick, cheap meal. Go before or after when there is a late-afternoon lull - a great time to have a meal before the crowds pick up again for dinner. However, it is worth noting that some of the most popular stalls on the island open for only a few hours a day because their food often sells out during lunch-time!

8. ORDERING FOOD LIKE A PRO

As a stall's menu is often displayed on a stall's signboard as numbered pictures, ordering a dish can be as easy as pointing at it. But here's how to do it like a local.

Eat Like a Local

First, address the hawker or stall assistant as Auntie/Uncle (no we are not all related in this tiny nation; Singaporeans address any person older than them as such, including strangers) or Boss/Miss. State the dish you want, the quantity, any condiment preference (no chilli/extra chilli/more noodles/less rice/no green onions/etc.) and if you're 'having here' or 'take-away'.

If in doubt, get help from any local in the queue who will probably be more than happy to answer a food-related question. And if you're too shy to do so, just point to the person in front of you, and say 'same as him/her'!

9. DIETARY RESTRICTIONS

Eating your way through Singapore's street food can be hard with dietary restrictions. While halal and vegetarian options are readily found in hawker centres to cater to the Muslim, Buddhist and Hindu populations here, other dietary needs such as kosher, gluten-free or peanut-free are virtually unheard of in these centres. As such, asking a hawker for such restricted options would unfortunately probably result in leaving the stall empty-handed. If need be, do check online to see what a dish is made of before visiting a centre as most hawkers may also probably not be willing to divulge ingredients in their secret recipes.

Restaurants, on the other hand, may be able to cater to specific restrictions. While gluten-free and vegan options are not usually available at middle-ranged restaurants here, more upscale restaurants and trendy cafes can cater to such requests, but it is best to check with them before-hand.

10. SELF-SERVICE

If a stall has a 'Self-Service' sign, it means that you have to collect your food yourself. These stalls take payment up front and require you to either hang around the stall and wait for your food, or to come back later to collect it. Asking the hawker how long the wait will be can help you decide which to do.

Stalls without a sign require you to provide your table number as they will deliver your food to you. They often serve dishes that require a longer time to cook. Payment is collected either upfront or when the food is delivered, depending on the stall.

11. CARRY CASH IN SMALL CHANGE

With dishes often costing less than $10 each, it is best to carry cash in smaller denominations to pay for your meal. Many locals know that paying with a $50 bill for a $4 plate will likely elicit displeasure from the stall auntie or uncle, or worse, the ire of a hungry queue if the auntie or uncle has to run to the next stall to obtain change for your large bill.

While there has been recent trials to introduce electronic payment options in hawker centres, cash is still the de facto mode of payment.

12. DO NOT TIP

Tipping is non-existent in Singapore's hawker centres, food courts and coffee shops. No matter how much you love the food, or are pleased with the service, tipping is not expected and any attempt will most likely be met with confusion.

As for restaurants and cafes, tips are included in the total bill as a 10% service charge. No fumbling over mental sums needed when the bill comes!

13. HALAL UTENSILS

If you order dishes from both a halal and non-halal stall, do remember to not mix the utensils! Under the Islamic law, halal food has stringent meal preparation rules to adhere to, such as no pork or lard or using only halal meat. Hence there is a need for Muslims to keep their halal food and utensils separate from non-halal items.

Halal plates and utensils are also returned to different cleaning stations and washed separately from the non-halal items. As such, they are coloured differently from the regular ones to avoid confusion. So, please do respect the Muslims' religious practices by using only using halal utensils when eating halal food.

14. (DON'T) RETURN YOUR TRAYS

While customers are encouraged to clear their tables and return their trays to the tray return stands after they are done, no one will bat an eyelid if you don't. Cleaners are employed in all centres and often spotted armed with a cloth and a cleaning cart, continuously clearing dishes and wiping tables down.

Recent initiatives to get customers to return their trays have ignited local debate, and surprisingly not due to the question of personal social responsibility. Instead, some say that cleaning up after themselves would help make cleaners' tiring jobs a little easier, while others believe that doing so would eventually deprive the cleaners of a job. Hawkers and cleaners themselves have also been slow to catch on, so time will tell if returning our trays becomes the norm.

15. DABAO

Prefer to eat in the cool comfort of your room instead of dining at the hawker centre? When you're ordering, tell the hawker 'take-away' or 'dabao' (pronounced ta-pao; a Singlish phrase of Mandarin origins meaning- to pack something). Or if you're buying from a Malay stall, say 'bungkus' (the Malay word for packet).

All stalls offer take-away options, and an extra 20cents is often charged to take-away the food in a disposable container. Be sure to grab the disposable utensils and packets of chilli or sauces only if needed!

16. OPEN HOURS

As hawker stalls set their open hours individually, open hours vary from stall to stall vary, even if they're located in the same hawker centre.

Eat Like a Local

Due to Singapore's multi-racial population, public holidays are observed during several religious or cultural celebrations. As a hawker stall's cuisine tends to reflect hawker's own culture, you may find some stalls closed depending on the public holiday.

For example, during the Chinese Lunar New Year, many Chinese stalls tend to close for a few days, while Hindu hawkers may do the same during Deepavali. During the month of Ramadan where Muslims observe fasting from sunrise to sunset, many Malay and Indian-Muslim stalls adjust their timings to open later to accommodate their fellow Muslim patrons.

So it is best to be prepared by either checking a stall's open hours online or to ask a local who would be able to advise you on its open hours during different public holidays and save you a trip down. And on the bright side, since Singapore is so small, even a trip to an unknowingly closed food stall is bound to have you chance upon another hidden gem of a stall nearby!

17. RESEARCH, RESEARCH, RESEARCH

Thanks to many a Singaporean's love affair with food, the internet has blossomed into a great place to find the best eateries. With almost religious fervour, both amateurs and professionals regularly create and update lists of the best spots to find a beloved dish.

While the internet has turned many a casual eater into food critics, do not be too quick to discount a seeming lack of credentials though. Many of these food bloggers' lists are actually revered by locals, and often worth a try. Food bloggers that have since risen to fame and post sound recommendations include Seth Lui, Lady Iron Chef, Miss Tam Chiak, DanielFoodDiary, The Halal Food Blog and Have Halal Will Travel.

For recommendations from an accredited site, do check out the yearly Michelin food guide which is a great place to suss out more than 200 places in Singapore serving great food, including hawker stalls.

Local websites worth a mention include Chope and HungryGoWhere, which are locally crowd-sourced guides to the best stalls, restaurants and bars to go classified according to different cuisines, budgets and locations. With comprehensive and more importantly, up-to-date information, these sites are extensively used by many locals and are a good resource for anyone to peruse.

Pro-tip: DO NOT use Yelp. Yelp may be popular in the United States but is rarely used here in Singapore. While it is still best to use all the resources mentioned earlier, the only other site with both an international user base and decent recommendations in Singapore, is TripAdvisor.

18. ONE-MICHELIN STAR STREET FOOD

For such a tiny country, Singapore has the honour of having 44 restaurants/stalls awarded Michelin-stars in 2019 and of the 37 restaurants that received one Michelin-star, a couple are actually hawker stalls. And the best news? You don't have to break the bank to try a one-Michelin star dish; the famous soya sauce chicken rice served at Hawker Chan in Chinatown Complex and Food Centre earned the title of the World's Cheapest Michelin-Star Meal at just $2 a plate!

19. A TRADITIONAL *KOPITIAM* BREAKFAST

Now that you know how and where to eat in Singapore, the next few tips will focus on quintessential local meals and dishes to try.

For many a Singaporean, there is no better breakfast than the simple traditional *kopitiam* breakfast of *kaya* toast, half-boiled eggs and a cup of coffee/tea. Available at most drink stalls in the mornings, kaya toast comprises of a thick spread of *kaya* jam (a coconut jam sometimes flavoured with pandan) and butter sandwiched between two slices of toasted bread. Often served with two intact soft boiled eggs, customers are expected to crack their eggs onto the plate themselves, before adding a little dark soya sauce and white pepper. The resulting runny mixture

Eat Like a Local

is often used as a dip for the kaya toast, and the simple meal finished off with a hot cup of *kopi* or *teh*.

Besides hawker centres and *kopitiams*, this breakfast can also be found in two home-grown chain cafes called **Ya Kun Kaya Toast** and **Killiney Kopitiam**. Variations of the humble kaya toast can be found in these chains, such as French Toast with Kaya, amongst other local breakfast dishes, and is popular with locals during breakfast and tea.

20. KOPI, TEH OR ME?

Craving a cup of coffee? Ditch the chain stores, and try ordering one from a drinks stall instead. Even in Singapore's year-round hot and humid weather, a piping hot cup of coffee and tea is a popular drink anytime during the day. Coffee shops tend to have just one drink stall, while hawker centres have almost one in each row of stalls. Often, you don't even have to move from your seat as drink stall assistants make their rounds around the tables to take orders. Pay them only when the drink is delivered and remember, that even with table service, no tip is needed.

Try starting with the basics- Kopi-O/Teh-O (black coffee/tea with sugar), Kopi-O Kosong/Teh-O Kosong (plain black coffee/tea) or a slightly more indulgent treat of Kopi Peng/Teh Peng (iced coffee/tea with condensed milk). Starting to get confused? You're not alone! Even after living in Singapore for my whole life, I have only just started to master ordering my favourite variations in my mid-twenties.

But if you're feeling adventurous, and willing to elicit a laugh (or maybe a frown if it's a grumpy auntie/uncle), try this! A quick google search on ordering kopi in Singapore will pull up several useful infographics that will teach you more than 10 different combinations, and hopefully, help you order your perfect cup of coffee or tea!

21. SWEET DRINKS ARE MADE OF THESE

Not a caffeine drinker? Try a myriad of local drinks instead. Many of them tend to taste sweet, catering to taste buds here and easily guzzled as the perfect antidote on a sweltering day. (Fun fact: Singapore has one of the highest incidences of diabetes among developed countries, a statistic so dire that the Prime Minister felt the need to address it in his annual National Day speech in 2017.)

Be sure to order at least one of these classic crowd favourites to enjoy with your hawker food. Sugarcane juice is the perfect thirst-quencher and is often freshly squeezed upon order. A sweet black drink made of sugar syrup and water, *Chin chow* is named after the slightly bitter tasting-herbal grass jelly that completes this drink. *Bandung* is a pretty pink mix of rose cordial syrup and either evaporated or condensed milk. Barley, water boiled with barley seeds, has a nutty taste and varying degrees of sweetness depending on the stall.

Tip: Try to get the fresh versions of these drinks. Some of these drinks have canned versions, and while still good, they really can't compare to a freshly-made cup.

22. LOCAL DESSERTS

Still in need of a sugar fix to wash down your greasy hawker meal? Like our drinks, we love our desserts sweet! Here are a couple of recommendations.

Cheng Tng, a refreshing clear soup with a variety of traditional ingredients such as dried longan, dates, barley, gingko nuts, lotus seeds and white fungus. Sweetened with rock sugar, it can be eaten both warm or chilled. *Ice Kachang* is a colourful concoction of syrup-drenched shaved ice, on a bed of *agar agar* (jelly), sweet corn, red beans and *attap chee* (palm seeds), and topped with condensed milk. Similarly, *Chendol* is also a shaved ice with red beans and jellies but drenched with palm sugar syrup and thick coconut milk. While I'm personally not a fan, *Chendol* is definitely worth a try as it made it to CNN'S list of 50 of the world's best desserts in 2018.

Unfortunately, they are not uniquely Singaporean, as variations of them can be found across South-East Asia, along with fierce Internet debates on their origins.

23. FAMOUS DOWNTOWN HAWKER CENTRES

As many tourist attractions, as well as the Central Business District, are located in downtown Singapore, these hawker centres are popular with both tourists and locals.

With unique old architecture, **Lau Pa Sat** is arguably the prettiest hawker centre in Singapore and famous for Satay, a skewered barbecued meat dish. It's best visited at night when the adjacent road, Boon Tat Street is closed off and transformed into Satay Street.

Featured on the movie Crazy Rich Asians, **Newton Food Market** is located near the shopping district of Orchard Road. Hence, dishes here a little pricier than usual so it's good to check the prices before ordering. Newton may be famous for its great seafood but is even more infamous for its numerous touts (See Tip 5: Choosing a Seat). So do choose your stall wisely!

Located near Chinatown, **Maxwell Food Centre** has been featured in countless food shows, and for good reason. It's home to some of the best stalls, such as the famous **Tian Tian Chicken Rice** and a plethora of others that even includes a British stall and a Peranakan & Eurasian stall. Do come armed with patience; it is often crowded, with long queues at the popular stalls.

Eat Like a Local

24. FAMOUS EASTERN HEARTLAND HAWKER CENTRES

Willing to venture a bit further out to less touristy areas? Like most Easties (East-side resident), we are probably biased, but mostly right, when we say the best food is found in the East. Here are heartland gems worth the trek out.

Old Airport Road Food Centre in Kallang has been around since 1973 and is now home to over 150 stalls. With several award-winning stalls having been around for decades, there is often a long wait of up to 30 minutes for the popular dishes. These include *char kway teow* (wok-fried flat noodles with shrimp, cockles and Chinese sausage), *lor mee* (broad noodles served in a thick dark gravy with varied ingredients) and *wonton mee* (Cantonese dry noodle dish with pork and dumplings).

Bedok is home to **Fengshan Market & Food Centre** (also known as Block 85), a favourite supper hangout for many East-siders. Supper staples to try are *bak chor mee* (minced meat noodles), pork porridge and traditional glutinous rice ball dessert.

Located on the eastern shore near the airport, **Changi Village Hawker Centre** is popular with many Easties for its old-Singapore charm, and army personnel due to nearby training camps. Nasi Lemak (classic Malay dish of coconut rice with fried sides of anchovies, egg and chicken wing or fish, and sambal), Satay bee hoon (noodles in peanut sauce) and fried chicken chop *hor fun* (flat rice noodles in a thick sauce) are instant crowd-pleasers to try.

(Pro-tip: Don't be fooled by the sleepy Changi Village vibe though, if you stay out late enough, you may spot a specific group of tourists out here for a different kind of late-night snack.)

Another famous hawker centre on the eastern shore is **East Coast Lagoon Food Village**, explored in Tip 43. Beachfront Dining.

Eat Like a Local

25. OTHER FAMOUS HEARTLAND HAWKER CENTRES

Still not convinced that East is best? Non-Easties will be happy to share these popular heartland haunts.

Only open in the evenings till late, **Chomp Chomp Food Centre** in Serangoon is the go-to spot for its famed barbecued sambal (fragrant chilli-based sauce) stingray, *Hokkien mee* (stir-fried noodles with seafood and sliced pork), carrot cake (not the American dessert, but a savoury dish cubed radish wok-fried with egg) and Orh Luak (fried omelette with starch and small oysters). With most food served to your table, do be prepared for long waits instead of long queues.

Nestled in one of Singapore's oldest housing estates, **Tiong Bahru Market** is a scenic walk away from the MRT station. packed on weekends, crowd favourites include *lor mee,* roasted meat (duck, pork, chicken) with rice and *chwee kueh* (steamed rice cake topped with salty, preserved radish and chilli).

One of the first few hawker centres built, **ABC Brickworks Market & Food Centre** near Queenstown is known for its traditional Chinese double-boiled soups (believed to be nourishing), *char siew* (barbecued pork) rice and *lontong* (also known as *sayur lodeh* in Javanese cuisine). A Malay stew of rice cakes and vegetables in a coconut gravy of spices, the *lontong* here is said to be the best on the island and is best enjoyed when topped with spicy *sambal* and serunding (fried coconut flakes).

26. SUPPER SPOTS

In a relatively safe city with accessible late-night public transport options, meeting up for supper (any meal after dinner qualifies) has become common, especially for younger Singaporeans. Having a meal later is also preferred for some eager to escape Singapore's sweltering heat during the day. While there are many coffee shops and restaurants that close late, these supper spots are frequented for their affordable, tasty eats.

Eat Like a Local

For many, Indian-Muslim and Malay cuisine rank high on our supper favourites. Nothing quite hits the spot like the reliable *prata*, *murtabak* (*prata* stuffed with spiced mutton, onion and sauce) or a hearty plate of *nasi/Maggi goreng pattaya* (fried rice or fried Maggi ramen noodles fully wrapped in a thin omelette.) Besides the prata places (see tip 22), other popular eating houses include **Spize Bedok** which closes at 3am, and **Adam Road Food Centre**, located near the Singapore Botanic Gardens with varying closing times for different stalls. Supper highlights at the latter include *sup kambing* (rich, stew-like soup with tender mutton chunks), *mee soto* (flavourful, spicy chicken broth with noodles, shredded chicken and bean sprouts) and *mee goreng* (fried noodles) served with cheese fries. [Pro-tip: This hawker centre is also famous for its *Nasi Lemak* and *Ayam Penyet* (an Indonesian dish of smashed fried chicken with rice), however, these stalls close earlier in the day)].

Want bite-sized dishes instead? For many hungry young Singaporeans out late, **Swee Choon Dim Sum Restaurant** in Jalan Besar offers the perfect post-clubbing dim sum fix. Open from 6pm to 6am, reservations are recommended if you want to sit inside the restaurant. Be sure to try the much sought-after Salted Egg Yolk Bun!

27. CHINATOWN

An ethnic enclave for Chinese culture, Chinatown is buzzing with shops, restaurants, bars and hawker centres. For a truly local experience, try visiting these three locally renowned hawker centres - **Hong Lim Market & Food Centre**, **Chinatown Complex Food Centre** and **People's Park Food Centre**. More popular with locals rather than tourists, there are a plethora of food choices so do look out for the longest queues! (See Tip 7. Queueing: A Singaporean Pastime)

If you prefer a quick introduction to Singapore's signature street food, **Chinatown Food Street** is a great place to easily try several cuisines in an iconic al-fresco dining area reminiscent of Old Chinatown. While prices here are a little more expensive than usual, it is a great spot to soak in Chinatown's busy ambience while people watching.

Eat Like a Local

The buzz continues late into the night Chinatown as some of the island's best bars are found here along the streets of Amoy Street and Ann Siang Hill (see Tip 46. Bottoms Up!)

28. KAMPUNG GLAM

Kampung Glam was historically the designated Malay-Muslim and Arab quarter and has since developed into a vibrant enclave of Malay culture and cuisine. Set against the backdrop of the impressive Sultan Mosque, a prominent restaurant to try in this halal food haven is **Zam Zam**, an Indian-Muslim restaurant famous for its *murtabak*, *prata* and *Nasi Biryani* (aromatic basmati rice dish topped with curry). Halal international cuisines popular with many Muslim locals here include Mediterranean, Swedish and Thai restaurants.

The area truly comes alive come dusk, with many places offering al-fresco dining late into the night. Do note that while Kampung Glam a relatively alcohol-free zone as alcohol is not served at halal establishments, some bars and restaurants along Haji

Lane and Arab Street do, making it a great spot for a relaxing night out. (See Tip 40. Haji Lane Hipsters)

29. LITTLE INDIA

As its name suggests, Little India is the culturally Indian district, home to business and vendors specialising in Indian commodities and food. Often bustling with crowds into the night, there are many Southern and Northern Indian restaurants to chance upon and try. However, you can't go wrong with exploring **Tekka Market,** which houses a wet market in the morning, shops and also a food centre, of which the Indian *rojak*, *biryani* and *thosai* are worth braving the crowds for.

Another dish people travel from all over the island to eat in the restaurants here is the fish head's curry, a spicy robust curry made with vegetables and of course the fish head itself, marinated in curry sauce. While it may be a sight to behold, brave locals love telling others how delectable parts of the head actually are, such as the eyeball and the cheek flesh.

Eat Like a Local

Pro-tip: While not a food centre, Mustafa Centre is a huge, iconic 24-hour shopping centre in Little India known for selling everything under one roof. While few have conquered mastering the maze of six levels, jostling in the crowd amongst the most eclectic mix of goods makes for a fun shopping experience!

30. MUST-TRY CHINESE DISH: CHICKEN RICE

Hainanese chicken rice holds a special place in most Singaporean's hearts and is often the first dish we miss when we're overseas. While chicken rice, like many other popular dishes, have ignited eternal food wars with Malaysia with both sides claiming it as their own, there's no denying that for many, chicken rice is synonymous with Singapore cuisine.

Created originally by Hainanese immigrants from China, chicken rice is the perfect combination of bite-sized pieces of white (steamed) or roasted poached chicken served on top oily, fragrant, flavourful rice that is the true measure of the chicken rice. Garnished with cucumber, and served with a bowl of chicken broth, locals swear by the chilli sauce and garlic that complete this beloved dish. While decent chicken rice can be found in every hawker centre, coffee shop and food court here, the following serve up plates worth writing home about.

Arguably the most famous of them all, **Tian Tian Chicken Rice** (see Tip 23. Famous Downtown Hawker Centres) serves long queues daily and was even featured by Anthony Bourdain on his travel show. For an indulgent treat, try **Chatterbox**, located in Mandarin Orchard Hotel, for a premium version of the dish in an upscale dining experience that patrons say is well worth the expensive price tag. And if you're looking for a true hidden gem, Delicious Boneless Chicken Rice tucked away in the lower level of **Katong Shopping Centre** serves delectable roasted chicken rice (side serving of chicken feet optional) that people wait up to 45min for.

Eat Like a Local

31. MUST-TRY MALAY DISH: NASI PADANG

Originally originating from Indonesia, and also common in Malaysia, *nasi padang* has since evolved into the definitive dish of the Singaporean Malay cuisine, a plate of steamed white rice with side dishes. Far from a simple rice dish, *nasi padang* requires hours of preparation to provide a small buffet of different food items for each customer to choose. Displayed tantalisingly in trays behind a window, customers typically point to the dishes they want as the stall's *mak cik* (Malay term for auntie) dishes a portion onto a plate of steamed rice.

Must-try items include *beef rendang* (spiced beef curry), *sambal goreng* (long beans, beancurd and fermented soybeans fried with a spicy paste) and *tahu telur* (fried egg tofu). If you're feeling particularly adventurous, try lemak siput seduk (sea snail stew), sotong hitam (squid in black ink) and my personal favourite, *paru goreng* (spicy fried beef lungs). While available at hawker stalls scattered throughout the island, it is best tried at **Hjh Maimunah Restaurant** in Kampung Glam. Up to an impressive 50 different dishes are served daily in this award-winning restaurant, guaranteeing long queue of hungry customers all day.

Pro-tip: Pricing is dependent on the dish and the stall's mak cik; meat and fish items tend to be more expensive than vegetables. The cost of a plate can easily add up so a couple of ways to keep it in check is to ask the price of the meat before adding it to your plate and to limit yourself to 2-4 side dishes. If in doubt, ask the person next to you in queue who would probably be glad to help recommend a couple of dishes.

32. MUST-TRY INDIAN DISH: ROTI PRATA

Although both northern and southern Indian food can be found in Singapore, cuisine originating from the South tends to be more popular. One such dish is the *Roti Prata*, with variations of it also being found within the region. This buttery pan-fried flatbread is a national favourite that transcends local racial lines; it's hard to find a Singaporean who would refuse a

Eat Like a Local

plate of such oily goodness! The hand-kneaded dough is made with ghee, and watching the cook (otherwise affectionately known as the *prata* -man) stretch, toss and fold the ghee-flavoured dough, before frying it on a griddle can be a treat in itself.

The simple *prata* has also evolved over the years, with many a *prata* shop now serving delectable variations of both savoury and sweet concoctions. Besides the *prata* kosong (plain *prata*), popular ones to try include egg *prata*, cheese *prata*, tissue *prata*, prata *prata*, and even ice-cream *prata*. It is often served with either sugar, sambal, dahl or curry depending on one's personal preference, so feel free to ask for a bit of each to try with your prata.

One of the most versatile dishes, *prata* is eaten at breakfast, lunch, teatime, dinner and even supper, as some stalls open late into the night. Although you can't go wrong with most *prata* stalls, popular haunts include **Mr & Mrs Mohgan**, **Al-Ameen Eating Houses**, **The Prata Place**, and my personal favourite- **Casuarina Curry.**

(Pro-tip: *Prata* tastes even better when eaten with just your hands! It's also common to order at least two *prata* and to wash it down with a cup of *Teh Tarik,* a pulled hot milk tea.)

33. MUST-TRY SINGAPOREAN DISH: CHILI CRAB

Widely endorsed as a national dish, chilli crab is easily found in seafood restaurants around the island. This iconic dish first became popular in the 1950s and comprises of mud crabs stir-fried in a thick sweet, yet savoury tomato and chilli-based sauce flecked with delicious stirred-in bits of egg.

Before you dig into the dish literally, be warned that this is a messy dish so do use the provided plastic gloves and aprons if provided. To enjoy the gravy, locals typically dip the side dish of fried *mantou* (small bread buns) into it, often while the buns are still hot.

With varying levels of sweetness and spiciness depending on the restaurant, most Singaporeans are divided on where the best chilli crab can be found. However, these three restaurants are safe bets for a

Eat Like a Local

delicious meal of chilli crabs. Serving a very mildly spicy gravy, **Jumbo Seafood** has been popular with both locals and especially tourists for years, with numerous outlets throughout the island. Originally a hawker stall, **No Signboard Restaurant** has several outlets serving quality chilli crabs that have kept many patrons coming back time and again. Touted to be the home of the very first chilli crab dish, **Roland Restaurant** has loyal customers who have patronized their restaurant for years, enjoying their slightly sweeter gravy.

Pro-tip: If available, do also try the pepper crab. Another iconic Singaporean dish, this version of crabs, wok-fried in a spicy black pepper paste, is also a favourite of many who prefer their crabs not doused in gravy.

34. EURASIAN FOOD

Once considered the fourth major ethnic group in Singapore, Eurasians now make up less than 1% of Singapore's total population. During Singapore's colonial days under the British, any European and

Asian intermarriage resulted in a Eurasian offspring, with the predominant mix being of the Portuguese and Malayan communities. Today, Eurasian cuisine has since developed from this pairing, with star dishes boasting influences from Malaya, Portugal and England.

Despite it being a tiny community with often fiercely guarded family recipes, Eurasian cuisine continues to live on commercially thanks to restaurants such as **Quentin's the Eurasian Restaurant** in Tanjong Katong and **Popo & Nana's delights**, a hawker stall in Maxwell that serves both Eurasian and Peranakan food. Dishes that are much loved by the Eurasians themselves include curry *debal* (also called curry devil by Eurasians; a very spicy curry traditionally cooked with leftover meats during Christmas), smore (rich beef stew) and *feng* (a spiced stew of diced pork and innards). Finish off your meal with a slice of Eurasian sugee cake, a sweet dense cake made with semolina flour, almonds and brandy, a quintessential treat at Eurasian celebrations.

(Pro-tip: Set aside an hour after your meal at Quentin's to explore the Eurasian Community House

Eat Like a Local

it is located at. Learn more about Eurasians unique to this region through exhibitions and archives detailing the contributions and struggles of this slowly disappearing community. Also the best Eurasian food is home-cooked so in the event a Eurasian person invites you over for a meal, do jump at it!)

35. PERANAKAN FOOD

Another small but established ethnic group in Singapore are the Peranakans, who have a distinct Peranakan or Nonya cuisine, reflective of their Chinese and Indonesian/Malaysian roots. Utilising largely Indonesian/Malaysian spices and cooking techniques with Chinese ingredients, the dishes to try include *ayam buah keluak* (a tangy bitter dish of tamarind paste and spices cooked with the seeds of a Kepayang tree and chicken), *laksa* (spicy coconut-based curry soup served with thick white noodles, fishcake, prawns and cockles) and *ngoh hiang* (spring rolls stuffed with minced pork and prawns). While there are several established restaurants in Singapore, the Katong district is a great place to start your Peranakan food journey.

Do remember to also give the Nonya *kueh* (cakes) a try! With primary ingredients such as coconut, pandan, tapioca and beans, these cakes are often home-made; popular ones include *kueh lapis* (rainbow-coloured layered cake) and *ondeh-ondeh* (green sweet balls covered in coconut).

36. INTERNATIONAL CUISINE

The local food scene has continued to benefit from globalisation, with an ever-increasing amount of international franchises thriving in Singapore. While it is now easy to find cuisines ranging from Brazillian to Greek, the most popular cuisines are still, not-surprisingly, from our Asian neighbours.

Thai food has been a firm favourite for years now, with a concentration of the most authentic stalls situated in **Golden Mile Complex** located in Kallang. Also known as 'Little Thailand', many stalls are run by Thai people themselves and frequent haunt of the Thai diaspora in Singapore.

Eat Like a Local

Japanese food has also long held a special place in the hearts of many Singaporeans, and Japanese cuisine is readily available throughout the island in many malls and hotels. Popular affordable chains include **Sushi Tei** and **Genki Sushi**, while others in the mid-to-high price range favoured by the young professional crowd include Tanuki Raw and **Teppei Japanese Restaurant**, an omakase-style restaurant that requires reservations weeks in advance! Truly extravagant Japanese dining options are also available, such as **Shoukouwa**, a 2-Michelin-starred restaurant which uses fresh fish flown straight in from Japan.

37. LOCAL SNACKS

By now, you have probably realized how much we Singaporeans love our food, and always in search of good eats. As such, snacks are also an integral part of Singapore's food culture, tiding us over until the next meal.

While recent years have brought in a lot of international franchises, many locals still love their familiar fried snacks found in **Old Chang Kee**, a chain store selling fried local foods such as fish-balls, chicken wings and curry puffs. Other snacks can be found in stand-alone stalls in hawker centres or at *kopitiam* drink stalls, or local bakeries. Popular Singaporean snacks to try include *pisang goreng* (deep fried banana), *epok-epok* (Malay curry puffs) and *you tiao* (fried dough fritters).

One snack that has been gaining in popularity is the salted egg fish skin/potato chips. With more home-grown brands now selling them in supermarkets, it is not hard to get your hands on a packet, but many locals and tourists from neighbouring countries still swear by **Irvins**, with outlets still garnering long queues each day.

38. FAST FOOD WITH A LOCAL TWIST

To embrace the local cuisine, many seasoned travellers would advise avoiding international fast food chains when in a foreign country. However, to

Eat Like a Local

truly eat like a local in Singapore, I would suggest trying fast food, especially with a local twist.

Singaporeans do really love their fast food, with outlets often packed at mealtimes. International chains such as **McDonald's** and **Burger King** often have country-specific menu items and seasonal specials reflective of local culture. Special in the past include the *nasi lemak* or *rendang* (Indonesian spicy meat dry curry) burger, as well as durian or *chendol* ice cream. With such interesting flavours available nowhere else in the world, it is definitely worth popping into a fast-food chain here just to check what is available.

(Pro-tip: Jet-lagged and hungry? McDonald's offers 24/7 island-wide delivery, a service especially used by young Singaporeans during an all-night study and school project sessions.)

39. WE LOVE OUR BUBBLE TEA

Bubble tea drinkers are a ubiquitous sight in Singapore because the younger generation of Singaporeans are obsessed with bubble tea (me included!). Once thought to be just a passing fad from the shores of Taiwan years ago, the bubble tea culture has grown and looks set to stay. Many famous names from around Asia have set up shop in Singapore and has proven to be so popular that every shopping mall in Singapore (thankfully!) houses at least one stall. Famous new franchises boast of snaking queues on opening day, while other long-standing brands boast of stores across the island. Popular brands to try include newer stores such as **Tiger Sugar**, **Playmade**, **HEYTEA** and **The Alley**, as well as established brands such as **Koi**, **Gong Cha**, and our very own local brand **LiHo Tea**.

With a plethora of options, don't hesitate to pick any of these stores and order a cup of bubble tea. Even though they are not as cheap as drink from a hawker stall, they are still relatively inexpensive and can be filling. Recommended flavours and toppings are often indicated on the menu, and you can rarely go wrong with them.

Fun fact: According to Mothership, a local community news website, the neighbourhood of Tampines is the unofficial capital of bubble tea with a whopping 14 stalls in the vicinity!

40. HAJI LANE HIPSTERS

Nestled in Kampung Glam (for more information, see Tip 28. K), there lies a street known for its quirky cafes, eclectic shops and graffiti murals (legal of course), in other words, a haven for Singapore's young hipsters. A stroll through the uncovered street of Haji Lane is best done in the late afternoon or evening when it's not as hot out, offering plenty of Insta-worthy photo opportunities. Do take a break-in of the cafes here offering healthy juices and local-inspired confectionaries to people watch!

Several bars along Haji Lane & adjacent Arab Street also offer great cocktails and good music, the perfect combination of a relaxing night out for many young locals. So, if that's your cup of tea, do check out **Bar Stories**, **Blu Jaz Cafe** and **Going Om**, great places to soak in the chill ambience of Haji Lane and unwind.

41. CAFE HOPPING CULTURE

In a city that is largely dependent on technology, it is not hard to understand why the younger generations of Singaporean are a social media savvy bunch. Combining that with an innate love of food, it is common to find many young Singaporeans flocking to the newest cafes (not to be confused with coffee shop, which is locally used when describing *kopitiams*) to post online about. Cafe-hopping, where one visits several cafes in a single outing, has fast caught on amongst them, due to a growingly affluent society.

Often serving fancy coffee and tea with latte art, and interesting pastries or food, cafes with unique decor and Insta-worthy menu items, are often the ones that last in the local cafe scene. However, with cafes constantly opening (and closing) throughout

Singapore from the downtown area to the heartlands, it is best to do a little internet research to find a cafe near you worth a visit (See Tip 17. Research, Research, Research). You are likely to be spoilt for choice, and even possibly be tempted to indulge in a little cafe-hopping of your own too!

42. PICTURE-PERFECT SPOTS

In highly urbanised Singapore, it is always a treat for us to dine in a more quiet, obscure location, especially when it's in a picture-perfect setting. If time, and transport permits, these few spots are worth braving the inaccessibility.

Set in a black and white colonial building and a former British military airbase, **Wheeler's Estate** in Seletar offers European cuisine in a quiet setting, that has become a popular local wedding venue too.

Surrounded by lush greenery, Dempsey Hill is home to several restaurants such as **P.S Cafe** that offer a peaceful respite from the bustling shopping district of Orchard Road just 5 min away.

And last but not least, as a die-hard Eastie, I love **Coastal Settlement** in Changi, which offers the perfect blast to the past with as a stand-alone restaurant decked in vintage-decor amidst towering heritage trees. (Plan to visit nearby Changi Village on the same trip, See Tip. 24: Famous Eastern Heartland Hawker Centres.)

And as always remember to research for any similar restaurants that may be newly opened before your trip (See Tip 17. Research, Research, Research).

43. BEACHFRONT DINING

Singapore may be an island but unlike our neighbours, our beaches are definitely nothing to write home about. However, nothing beats a meal with a sea breeze, so here are a couple of areas locals frequent.

It may not be the most accessible area by public transport, but **East Coast Lagoon Food Village** on East Coast Beach is a still a bustling dinner spot, in sheer testament to its good food. With both halal and non-halal stalls offering similar *Zi Char* dishes (affordable mixed dishes served family-style), this spot is popular for big feasts amongst friends and family of different races looking for a seafood treat. Other must-tries include *satay*, *popiah* (fresh spring roll) and *char kway teow*. To complete the experience, factor time in for a short relaxing stroll in the beach park after to check out other restaurants here too.

For a more upscale experience, Sentosa is the place to go. An even smaller island South of Singapore, Sentosa is a pretty, manicured holiday island with beaches, attractions and activities for all to enjoy. The beachfront bars and restaurants here are a highlight, with many young locals and expats thronging the former. **Tanjong Beach Club** is the place to be seen, with food served on loungers and cocktails aplenty. **Coastes** has a more romantic, laid-back feel, and with a wide menu of salads, burgers, pasta and pizza, it makes a perfect dinner spot to catch the sunset.

And if you're looking for a meal, you'll remember for years to come, try **Ocean Restaurant by Cat**

Cora, located in the SEA Aquarium. While the food is not exactly local and neither is it beachfront, fine-dining on Mediterranean-Californian fusion food in the company of fish, manta rays and sharks is definitely worth the splurge in Southeast Asia's only underwater aquarium dining experience.

44. IT'S TIGER TIME

One of Singapore's most famous exports, Tiger Beer is a home-grown brand of beer that is the pride of many older Singaporean drinkers. First brewed in 1932, Tiger Beer has stood the test of time and is now a staple at bars, restaurants and even hawker centres and *kopitiams* here. For a truly local experience, do order a bottle at your next hawker or *kopitiam* meal. Pairing it with a greasy plate of hawker food is recommended, especially since they tend to be sold cheaper there.

Eat Like a Local

45. BREWERIES

With the rich nightlife scene in Singapore, breweries have been on the rise offering locals a refreshing change from the many international beer brands that dominate the market. And despite being a small nation, there are surprisingly enough variations in the different breweries bound to please different crowds.

For a brewery with a view, head to **Level33**, the highest urban microbrewery in the world, offering contemporary spins on classic beer. Veterans on the local brewery scene, **RedDot BrewHouse** offers their unique Green Monster Lager, a hit during St. Patrick' Day Celebrations. New to the scene, **Little Island Brewing Co** offers interesting brews amidst a laid back vibe at Changi Village (see Tip 24. for more information about Changi Village).

46. BOTTOMS UP

For a conservative country with many rules and almost exorbitant alcohol prices, Singapore still manages to offer a thriving dinner and bar scene frequented by working professionals. Amoy Street, Ann Siang Hill and Club Street, all located in the Chinatown district, come alive in the evening, with roads closed off to make way for the human traffic in these narrow roads. Amongst the historic colourful shophouses that line the street are contemporary restaurants and bars that offer a vibrant ambience with many food and drink options.

Places worth a mention in this district include **Native Bar** voted one of Asia's Best Bars, **Operation Dagger**, a hidden underground speakeasy, and **The Coconut Club**, a restaurant serving a slightly upscale twist on the classic *nasi lemak* dish.

Eat Like a Local

47. ROOFTOP BARS

Many Singaporeans know that the best way to take in Singapore's gorgeous skyline is from high up with a drink in hand. As such, rooftop bars have sprouted up all over downtown Singapore in the past decade or so, allowing everyone a chance to bask in the glistening Singapore city lights. With many options available, here are three bars that guarantee you an amazing view.

Kinki Restaurant + Bar, a Japanese joint with an edgy urban touch, is a popular happy-hour spot both the locals and expat working professionals circles. Although only located on the roof of the three-story Customs House, this watering hole still offers a dramatic view of the iconic Marina Bay waterfront, framed by nearby skyscrapers that tower over the restaurant/bar.

CÉ LA VI Restaurant & SkyBar is a luxurious restaurant on the 57th level of the iconic Marina Bay Sands SkyPark. While meals here are pricey, you may prefer to save this for an after-dinner spot to enjoy a hand-crafted cocktail while taking in the breath-taking views of the bay and the city.

I may be biased but I saved the best, and my personal favourite rooftop bar, for last. Located on the 63rd story of the 1 Raffles Place building, **1-Altitude is** the highest bar in Singapore offering 360° panoramic views of the city. There is a cover charge to enter but is well worth it in my opinion, just to enjoy a drink against an unparalleled, spectacular view of the Singapore cityscape.

Do note that most rooftop bars do have a dress code of smart casual, so do put away your flip-flops and shorts on a night out in downtown Singapore.

48. NIGHTLIFE

For many clubbers in Singapore, a night out clubbing at Clarke Quay was a rite of passage once they turned 18. A lively, exciting district, Clarke Quay is the definitive clubbing district and is home to many restaurants and bars too. This place is packed during weekend nights, and despite the club scene, makes a fun dinner spot for even families looking to soak in the fun atmosphere. As restaurants and bars here do change hands quite often, it's best to walk around to look for a restaurant or bar that suits your fancy on a night out here.

49. SPLURGING IN THE MOST EXPENSIVE CITY IN THE WORLD

With almost 200,000 millionaires, and a couple of famous billionaires that call Singapore home, eating like a local could also mean splurging like a local millionaire. Reportedly the most expensive city in the world, Singapore also presents luxurious fine-dining experiences that may be well worth the splurge.

Two such restaurants that are definitely worth the splurge are **Les Amis** and **Odette**, both offering French cuisine and scoring three-Michelin stars in 2019. The latter was also voted the best restaurant in Asia in 2019 and a meal here would set you back a couple of hundred dollars. Despite the high prices, these restaurants are almost always fully reserved so do book a table in advance.

50. EAT WITH A LOCAL

And for the final tip, the best way to eat like a local is to eat with a local. The only thing Singaporeans love more than our local cuisine is sharing about it. So if possible, sign up for a walking food tour to have someone show you the best spots or even better still, strike up conversations with locals you meet, such as taxi drivers, hotel staff, or people you share a table with at a hawker centre. While Singaporeans rarely make the first move in interacting with a stranger, most will be more than happy to share once you initiate a conversation, especially about food.

After all, that's how I met my husband - who was once just a clueless tourist who asked for help in finding the best chicken rice in Singapore, but now a fellow Singaporean food aficionado.

READ OTHER BOOKS BY CZYK PUBLISHING

Greater Than a Tourist- St. Croix US Birgin Islands USA: 50 Travel Tips from a Local by Tracy Birdsall

Greater Than a Tourist- Toulouse France: 50 Travel Tips from a Local by Alix Barnaud

Children's Book: *Charlie the Cavalier Travels the World* by Lisa Rusczyk

Eat Like a Local

Follow *Eat Like a Local* on Amazon.

Made in the USA
Coppell, TX
19 November 2023